Legacy from the Past

Library of Congress Catalogue Card Number: 73-173788
Colonial Williamsburg ISBN: 0-910412-97-9 (hardbound)
0-910412-98-7 (softbound)

Printed in the United States of America

FIFTH PRINTING, 1978

A Portfolio of Eighty-eight Original Williamsburg Buildings

Legacy from the Past

THE
COLONIAL WILLIAMSBURG
FOUNDATION
Williamsburg, Virginia

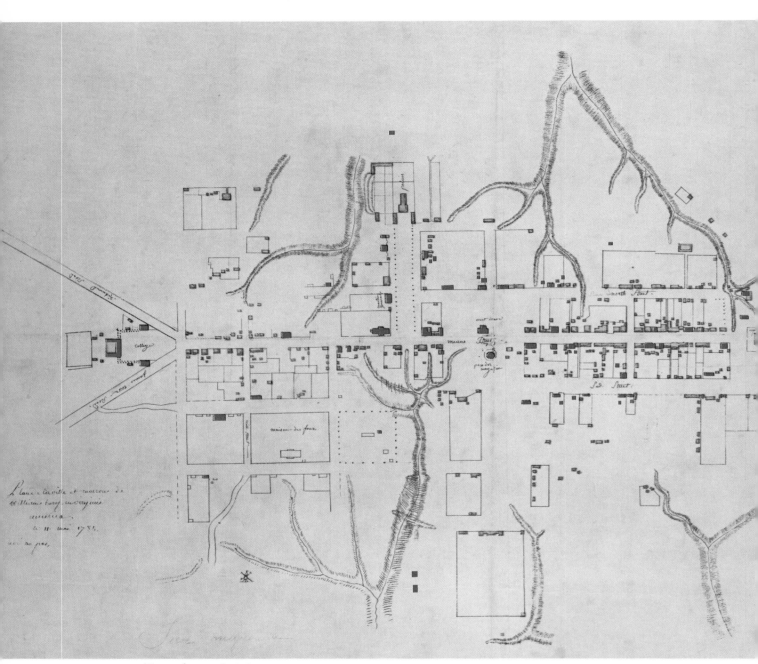

Frenchman's Map

A plan showing the buildings of Williamsburg, probably
made by a French army officer for the purpose of billeting
troops after the siege of Yorktown in 1781. The original,
dated 1782, is in the archives of the Earl Gregg Swem
Library of the College of William and Mary.
The eighty-eight original buildings that survive today
are here indicated in red.

"THE PLAN OF VIRGINIA'S SECOND COLONIAL capital deserves . . . recognition as the basic platform on which the third dimension of architecture could take form gracefully and with full visual effect. This approach to environmental design is a great lesson Williamsburg has to teach—that only where streets, open spaces, and building sites are conceived of, not as an abstract pattern but as part of a three-dimensional concept, can cities be beautiful as well as functional. *It is not the exact architectural styles or details of the buildings or the precise form of the city plan that should be imitated, but this fundamental approach to the problem of creating urban spaces defined by buildings of pleasing size, materials, and proportions.** The modern generation of urban designers wrestling with the problems of great cities might ponder the lesson of Williamsburg and find much to learn from this small town of the Virginia Tidewater."

> —JOHN W. REPS in *Tidewater Towns:
> City Planning in Colonial Virginia
> and Maryland*

---

*Italics added.

5

Courthouse of 1770, with the 1809 Norton-Cole House and the
1769 steeple of Bruton Parish Church in the background.

Legacy from the Past

IN 1699, when Williamsburg began its life as one of America's first planned cities, a small settlement had existed here for nearly seventy years. From the Wren Building of the College of William and Mary, whose cornerstone had been laid four years earlier, the new city plan stretched eastward for a mile. Within the limits of its generous scale and design, scores of sturdy buildings rose along the streets and greens of the colonial capital. A remarkable number of them survive, one — the Wren Building — being even older than the city itself.

In all, eighty-eight of these original buildings from the eighteenth and early nineteenth centuries have withstood the toll exacted by fire, destruction, and decay. Without them there would have been no restoration of Williamsburg. It was the prospect of the preservation of these buildings and their dramatic historical significance that captured the imagination and held the interest of the Reverend W. A. R. Goodwin, former rector of Bruton Parish Church, and Mr. John D. Rockefeller, Jr., whose combined vision saved the major portion of the eighteenth-century town.

It is important to remember that Mr. Rockefeller launched his ambitious preservation program in Williamsburg because the city's surviving buildings had been familiar scenes to great leaders during a critical period of our history. Throughout his sixteen years as a burgess, Washington was frequently seen in the tavern public rooms, as a dinner guest at the Peyton Randolph House, at Bruton Parish Church, and just before Yorktown in his headquarters at the George Wythe House. Patrick Henry, a familiar figure in Williamsburg prior to the Revolution, was the first governor of the new commonwealth, and occupied the Governor's Palace. Jefferson studied in the Wren Building and Wythe House, lodged in Market Square Tavern, and was the last governor to live in the Palace. George Mason, "reluctant statesman," walked Duke of Gloucester Street and pondered the language of the Virginia Declaration of Rights and the first state constitution. The Byrds and the Carters, the Randolphs and the Nelsons mingled with the Wallers and the Powells, the Ludwells and the Taliaferros, the Blairs and the Galts.

Together they created a precious legacy, the visible symbols of which are the old buildings. These men were the leaders in a vibrant period in the life of this community and, many of them, in the organization of the nation itself. But for their presence here this restoration would lack its outstanding appeal.

The surviving historic buildings of Williamsburg are considerably more in number than is generally realized. They form a major portion of the important structures standing here around the middle of the eighteenth century. The earliest were familiar to such builders of the Virginia colony as Commissary James Blair, planter William Byrd, and Governor Alexander Spotswood, just as they were later to the giants of Virginia's revolutionary era.

The eighty-eight original buildings illustrate a

Ludwell-Paradise House, before restoration, its original masonry in excellent condition.

broad range of eighteenth- and nineteenth-century structures indigenous to the Tidewater: from simple dairies and smokehouses to dignified residences that reflect varying degrees of affluence, and from the stately church and college buildings to the practical and orderly designs of courthouse, magazine, and gaol. These originals include thirty-eight residences, eight public buildings, thirty-six outbuildings, two taverns, and four shops.

All of these buildings are located throughout and adjacent to the Williamsburg Historic Area—which is designated as a historic landmark by the Commonwealth of Virginia and is recorded as a registered national landmark by the National Park Service of the United States Department of the Interior.

One of the most interesting and important buildings is Bruton Parish Church. The parish, still an active one, was established in 1674, and the present structure dates from 1715.

Other of the more important buildings are open to the public, though most of them are occupied by

A portion of the Virginia Declaration of Rights adopted in Williamsburg in 1776. This document is largely the work of the scholarly George Mason of Gunston Hall.

Duke of Gloucester Street during the 1890s, its buildings much
as they were when Mr. John D. Rockefeller, Jr., first visited the city.

A view of the interior of an old
frame wall during the restoration of
Wetherburn's Tavern.

employees of the Colonial Williamsburg Foundation, all of whom lead active professional and social lives within the "museum" itself. The buildings were acquired in various ways, many by purchase from the owners subject to a life tenancy. Under this arrangement the houses were sold to Colonial Williamsburg, carefully restored, and then occupied as residences by their former owners. Some of these life tenants are direct descendants of the original owners. Even now, more than forty years after the beginning of the restoration, life tenants live in a number of the houses. Their spirit of cooperation and support was supplemented by that of other local citizens, with the result that the foundation came into possession not only of the original buildings but of other important properties as well.

The work of preservation and restoration, begin-

10

Duke of Gloucester Street today, after more
than forty years of the work of the restoration.

ning in 1928 with the Wren Building and focusing
always on the original buildings, continues. Henry
Wetherburn's Tavern, for example, was acquired by
long-term lease from its present-day owners, the
Bucktrout-Braithwaite Memorial Foundation. It was
restored in 1968, two and a quarter centuries after
its doors opened in the 1740s.

Restoration of each individual building presented
a different but always complex problem demanding
the most careful handling of antique materials. Some
restorations required less work than others. Many
brick structures, for example, weathered the years so
well that their masonry walls stood virtually intact.
Among these are the Courthouse of 1770, Bruton
Parish Church, the Public Records Office, Lightfoot
House, Norton-Cole House, Ludwell-Paradise House,
Wythe House, Gaol, Palmer House, Brush-Everard

Typical brickwork in an original
Williamsburg building.

11

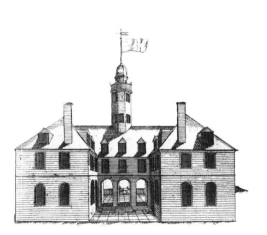

Details from the "Bodleian Plate," a copperplate engraving of about 1740, discovered by Miss Mary F. Goodwin, a Colonial Williamsburg research worker, at Oxford University. It was later given to Mr. John D. Rockefeller, Jr., by the curators of the Bodleian Library at Oxford. Renderings of the Capitol (above) and the Governor's Palace assisted in the reconstruction of these important buildings.

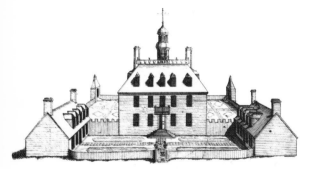

Kitchen, Greenhow-Repiton Office, and the Wren Building, President's House, and the Brafferton at the College of William and Mary.

The preservation of others involved more substantial repair work. New framing timbers would be necessary in one house, replacement weatherboarding, roofing, or trim in another. In each case original material was preserved intact whenever possible.

The concept of restoring the major portion of the old colonial capital also included the decision to replace a number of historically important buildings that had disappeared. Without them the educational significance of Williamsburg as the scene of decisive events in our past would have been incomplete. Thus such buildings were reconstructed on their original foundations with the aid of careful archaeology and voluminous documentary evidence — wills, deeds, journals, eyewitness accounts, early drawings, and even photographs. The best known of these reconstructed buildings are the Governor's Palace and the Capitol, both shown on a detailed engraving of about 1740 discovered at Oxford University and known as the Bodleian Plate. Thomas Jefferson's sketches of the plan of the Palace, whose details assisted our interior reconstruction, illustrate the value of such documentary evidence. For practical evidence, the original buildings themselves provided a vast catalogue of characteristic and distinctive details of doors and doorways, chimneys, fireplaces and mantels, cornices and dormers, paneling, flooring, stairs, windows, shutters, brickwork, and roof shapes.

Fortunately, most of the surviving buildings are of major importance — larger dwellings and public buildings. (The great loss over the years occurred in small wooden outbuildings, though the variety of remaining examples of these give us an accurate guide to the eighteenth-century appearance of the entire town.) The residences are comfortable but not ostentatious. They bear little comparison to the large and luxurious homes in contemporary rural England or to those in other colonial capitals and cities. Their proportions are pleasing, their ornamental details are conventional, readily adaptable, easily comprehended.

The perceptive visitor today, viewing the remaining buildings, will make his own discoveries: a small frame dairy in the shadow of the two-story Archibald Blair House—the style and scale of each merging unaffectedly with the other; the four outbuildings grouped comfortably about the handsome Powell-Waller House; the weathered well house close behind the George Reid House; and the range of size and form represented in the Magazine, the Gaol, and the Market Square Tavern.

This kinship of design and atmosphere derives neither from age nor accident. Indeed, the relationship of houses to each other, to the public structures, and to the greens and streets is a visual lesson in urban development bequeathed to us by two governors and planners, Francis Nicholson and Alexander Spotswood. The enduring validity of these principles is emphasized by the ease and grace with which the privately owned 1858 Bowden-Armistead House sits between the early colonial Bruton Parish Church and the John Blair House of mid-eighteenth-century date. The concern of early planners with preserving vistas and open spaces is apparent to the visitor. Equally important were their initial stipulations that required residential lots of about half an acre, fencing, houses set back six feet from the Duke of Gloucester Street, and minimum building dimensions.

One of our primary concerns in the restoration program has been to protect this atmosphere generated by the original plan—a sense of appropriateness and balance that clings not only to the surviving eighty-eight buildings but is amplified by the im-

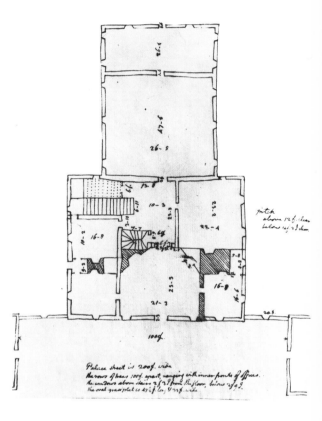

Thomas Jefferson's plan of the Palace, possibly drawn during his first term as governor when he resided in the building. (Reproduced with the permission of the Massachusetts Historical Society, which owns the original.)

13

portant reconstructions. Coming into this setting from the hectic pace of crowded cities, today's visitor easily grasps the intention of the planners. For even at its busiest, the Historic Area of Williamsburg reflects the spacious and tranquil nature of their vision.

From the first, Mr. Rockefeller perceived that of all the colonial capitals Williamsburg offered the best opportunity to transform an entire small town into a "living museum" set apart from a complex of modern buildings. His decision did not merely save the original buildings and raise others on their old foundations. It gave new direction to the historic preservation movement in America, which prior to Williamsburg had been characterized by two separate currents: the preservation of individual structures with strong historical associations, and the preservation of buildings distinguished by historic architectural qualities. In Williamsburg these currents dramatically converged.

In many other old American cities the patterns of preservation have taken appropriately different forms. Busy modern cities like Annapolis, Charleston, New Orleans, Boston, Savannah, or Philadelphia have encountered circumstances and problems different from those of Williamsburg. Yet the objective of saving and actively using historic areas is ours in common.

Colonial Williamsburg has always viewed its opportunity as unique, and though related closely to the work of other preservation endeavors, an undertaking secure in the validity of its original conception. The Colonial Williamsburg Foundation has supplied work, advice, and enthusiastic support for preservation efforts throughout much of the nation. But we have done so without altering our own initial purpose to develop the Historic Area as a living museum of eighteenth-century life.

In the following pages, simply and with a mini-

14

Gardens

Furnishings

History and Heritage

Working Crafts

Architecture is only one of the six basic appeals that attract visitors from all parts of the world. The other appeals are Williamsburg's gardens and greens, furniture and furnishings, preservation research, including archaeology, working crafts, and history and heritage.

Preservation Research

mum of comment (because we believe they speak for themselves), we present in a portfolio the original buildings. They combine to form one of Williamsburg's six basic appeals—architecture and the surviving town plan. The other five appeals, any one of which would constitute a cultural and educational landmark on its own, are the re-created eighteenth- and nineteenth-century gardens and greens, a uniquely extensive program of working crafts, the important collection of authentic seventeenth-, eighteenth-, and nineteenth-century furniture and furnishings, a broad and comprehensive program of preservation research, and our interpretation of the historical heritage of eighteenth-century Virginia.

15

The significance of the entire Williamsburg program, in which the original buildings play such a prominent role, is suggested in an eloquent statement by the noted historian Julian P. Boyd:

"Our historic shrines, our parks, our restorations, our pageants, and our monuments constitute a vast textbook across the land, wherein millions of people may deepen their experience, renew their acquaintance with the roots of their institutions, and occasionally encounter those rare moments of understanding and insight that regenerate our strength."

In this spirit Colonial Williamsburg treasures its original buildings as the most precious assets that have been entrusted to it. These old buildings are a *legacy from the past*; they are national heirlooms that recall a vital part of our heritage.

—CARLISLE H. HUMELSINE
President, The Colonial
Williamsburg Foundation

A Portfolio of Eighty-eight Original Williamsburg Buildings

- ■ PUBLIC BUILDINGS
- ■ RESIDENCES
- ■ OUTBUILDINGS
- ■ OFFICES
- ■ STORES AND SHOPS
- ■ TAVERNS
- ■ DETAILS

This portrait of the Reverend James Blair, founder and first president of the College of William and Mary, has been attributed to Charles Bridges. It must have been painted sometime after Bridges came to Virginia from England in 1735 and before Blair's death in 1743. At *left*, in enlargement, the artist's rendition of the Wren Building as it appears in the background of the painting.

The Public Buildings

Since eighteenth-century Williamsburg was a government town until the last months of the Revolution, its most important structures were public buildings. The variety of these which have survived indicates the vital purposes they served. These buildings housed virtually all government functions for a colony that stretched westward to the Mississippi and northward to the Great Lakes. The twentieth-century existence of eight of them was largely responsible for Mr. John D. Rockefeller, Jr.'s decision to restore the city.

The Wren Building was restored to the appearance it had after 1716. It survives as the oldest academic building in America.

The President's House of the College of William and Mary, built in 1732, damaged by fire while occupied by French officers in 1781 following the siege of Yorktown, and restored five years later with funds supplied by the French government.

The Brafferton Indian School, built in 1723, housed Indian boys brought to Williamsburg to be educated in the ways of the white man. The experiment was of limited success.

The Magazine, storehouse for the colony's arms, was designed by Governor Alexander Spotswood. Lord Dunmore, the last royal governor, enraged Virginians by secretly removing powder from the building one night in April 1775. Armed volunteers led by Patrick Henry marched toward Williamsburg and forced payment for the powder.

Public Gaol, one of the city's earliest buildings, with the Capitol overlooking it from the right background. Opened to receive its first prisoners in 1704, the surviving portion served as city jail until 1910. Among the many common criminals held here for trial or punishment were some not so common: members of Blackbeard's pirate crew and, during the Revolution, British Governor Henry Hamilton, known as the "hair buyer."

Courthouse of 1770 on Market Square, almost surrounded by original buildings on every hand. The original brickwork of the Courthouse is virtually intact.

Public Records Office, built to house the colony's records in 1748 after a disastrous fire destroyed the Capitol the year before. The pedimented, molded-brick doorway is quite similar to that of the nearby James River plantation house, Carter's Grove.

Many of Williamsburg's residents in the colonial era, both prominent and uncelebrated, lie today in Bruton Parish churchyard. Some of their tombstones are shown at left. Four periods in the history of this active Episcopal church are shown above: The south transept of 1715, the chancel (foreground) of 1750-1752, the churchyard wall of 1754, and the steeple of 1769.

24

Bruton's steeple was built by the local contractor, Benjamin Powell.
It houses an old bell, cast in Whitechapel, England, in the foundry that produced
the famous Liberty Bell in Philadelphia. Given to the church in 1761 by
James Tarpley, the bell was rung to celebrate the signing of the Treaty of Paris
in 1783, and on other significant occasions. Today, it continues to call
townspeople and visitors to worship as it has for more than 200 years.

Residences

The surviving original homes are remarkable for their number, variety, and condition. Though less expensively built than the city's public buildings, often of more perishable materials, thirty-eight of them have survived. Fortunately, these range from simple cottages to good-sized residences, and include several put to commercial as well as to residential use.

Left. The eighteenth-century residence of the Geddy family, prominent jewelers, silversmiths, and gunsmiths in Williamsburg. James Geddy, Jr., perhaps the most famous of the Geddy family, lived and worked here from 1760 to 1777.

Travis House. The section on the right dates from about 1763. Additions at the left were made successively into the early nineteenth century.

Peyton Randolph House from the rear. Several eighteenth-century additions resulted in an unusual roof line. This was the home of Peyton Randolph for most of his life including his years of leadership in the Virginia legislature, and of his service as president of the First Continental Congress.

An unusual view of the early nineteenth-century brick portion of the Norton-Cole House, on Duke of Gloucester Street at Market Square.

Nelson-Galt House, a typical small Williamsburg home on historic Francis Street, was for the last half of the eighteenth century the property of the eminent Nelson family of Yorktown, which included Thomas Nelson, a Revolutionary governor of Virginia and a signer of the Declaration of Independence.

Alexander Craig House, an eighteenth-century
example of a combined residence and saddler's
shop. The shop was at the right.

Palmer House, built between 1756 and 1760. In later years it was put to various uses. *Right.* A view of the "putlog holes" of the Palmer House. (The holes left by scaffolding timbers were not filled with bricks when builders left the job and are now vacant.)

Moody House, a rare example of a Williamsburg saltbox design. It was built before 1750 and altered several times, reaching its present appearance by 1782.

The handsome Ludwell-Paradise House of about 1740, an unconventional design featuring a depth of two rooms on the first floor, with a one-room depth above. The brickwork of the upper floor is different from that below, though the house was built in a single stage.

Bassett Hall, an eighteenth-century residence once owned by a kinsman of Martha Washington. It was built about 1760 adjacent to the town limits, where it still stands.

Lightfoot House began life as two "tenements" early in the eighteenth century. At that time a tenement was a building originally constructed for the purpose of renting. About 1750, after major alterations, it became a large family residence.

33

Semple House, a forerunner of the Federal style. Thomas Jefferson is believed to have designed the house.

Nicolson House. Its early section
(to the right) dates from about 1750,
with later additions.

Bracken House, a
typical small residence,
one room deep.

A closeup view of the original weatherboarding of the Benjamin Waller House, fastened with rose-headed nails.

Benjamin Waller House, with its original lightning rod. Except for three lower boards, the weatherboards are original on this elevation.

William Lightfoot House, a fine example of a gambrel roof, a style introduced in Williamsburg about 1750. The house is in a neighborhood of many other surviving eighteenth-century buildings.

Orrell House. Gambrel roofed like the William Lightfoot House, this small dwelling could fit perfectly into a twenty-eight-foot cube. The original frame residence apparently had no shutters in the eighteenth century.

George Reid House, an example of asymmetrical design. One interior and one exterior chimney resulted in one window to the left of the doorway and two windows to the right. The builder, George Reid, a merchant, was an ensign in the Revolutionary militia and secretary of the local Society of Freemasons.

St. George Tucker House is an unusual example of Tidewater domestic architecture. Dating from the last decade of the eighteenth century, it is one of the more important later houses in Williamsburg. Tucker, a lawyer and judge known as "the American Blackstone," was the second professor of law at the College of William and Mary.

Tucker's agreement with the painter Jeremiah Satterwhite in 1798 specified all colors to be used on the house: straw color, yellow ochre, chocolate, dark brick color, Spanish brown, stone color, and pure white. These paints were matched exactly through paint investigations of the building and are applied to the house today. The agreement for painting the house was signed by Tucker and witnessed by Mrs. E. H. Dunbar, a resident of the nearby Wythe House.

Robert Carter House, which dates from the late 1740s, once served Governor Dinwiddie as a temporary residence while the Palace was under repair. The house plan, unique in Williamsburg, features an **L**-shaped entrance hall. Its stair, several mantels, and chair rails are original, and it has the only surviving eighteenth-century plaster cornice in Williamsburg.

Brush-Everard House, part of which dates from 1717–1719, is of rare design. The chimneys were built on the rear of the house to provide for the wings added later. The brick kitchen on the left is also an original eighteenth-century building.

The Coke-Garrett House is made up of four sections covering the years from the mid-eighteenth century to 1837, but the residence today portrays its nineteenth-century appearance.

The story-and-a-half west wing existed by 1755. The railing of the porch (one of the few eighteenth-century porches remaining in Virginia) complements the "Chinese Chippendale" stair railing of the interior.

The central section of two-and-a-half stories was added by the Garrett family about 1837. The unusual spaciousness of the well-lighted rooms is due to the plan, which is only one room deep.

This small eastern wing was moved to its present location after 1837. The wing itself dates to the late eighteenth century.

This building dates from 1810–1820 and in 1862 was serving as Dr. Robert M. Garrett's office, from which he treated both Federal and Confederate wounded after the battle of Williamsburg.

41

Charlton House, a fine residence, almost directly across the
street from the famous Raleigh Tavern, on a lot once owned by
William Byrd II of Westover. It was built after 1740.

The Wythe House was designed and built after 1750 by Richard Taliaferro, who gave it to his son-in-law, George Wythe, first professor of law in an American college and Thomas Jefferson's law tutor. The house owes much of its distinction to its geometrical system of proportion, which won its reputation as one of the more handsome of Williamsburg's houses.

Ewing House, a late eighteenth-century combination of residence and shop, was owned by a Scottish merchant, Ebenezer Ewing. Almost all its original framing has survived and the interior stair, some doors, and most floors are original.

Dr. Barraud House, originally built one room deep, was altered to its present form later in the eighteenth century. It was owned by Dr. Philip Barraud, a soldier of the Revolution who later studied medicine at the University of Edinburgh.

John Blair House, its earliest portion shown to the right. Its expansion resulted in two doors opening on Duke of Gloucester Street, an unusual arrangement. A later shed addition was built at the rear. An early owner was John Blair, Jr., nephew of the Reverend James Blair.

The stately Taliaferro-Cole House, from its rear or southern elevation. This portion was built between 1815 and 1830 as an addition and enlargement to the original eighteenth-century section.

Tayloe House, one of three notable homes associated with the
Tayloe family that survive to the present day. This house was
built by James Carter, a surgeon and apothecary, and sold in 1759
to John Tayloe, a member of the Council. Tayloe, at the time, had
just completed the elegant stone mansion, Mt. Airy, in Richmond
County. The family also owned the famous Octagon House in
Washington, D.C.

Archibald Blair House. The colorful hues of this home are based on the investigations of the original paint.

Powell-Waller House. This portion was built in the third quarter of the eighteenth century as an addition to a much earlier brick portion in the rear. It was once owned by the local builder, Benjamin Powell.

The Quarter, a picturesque survivor
of the early nineteenth century. This
tiny cottage is now in use as a guest house.

Timson House, an unrestored
eighteenth-century small dwelling. A
house stood on this site as early as 1717.

Redwood Ordinary, an unrestored
small residence of the early nineteenth century.

Bowden-Armistead House, a Greek Revival
example built in 1858 of pressed brick imported
from Baltimore. The land was owned by Bruton
Parish Church until purchased by Lemuel J.
Bowden, a onetime mayor of Williamsburg.
Robert Armistead purchased the house and
property in 1875. It still remains in the family
today as the home of his grandson,
Judge Robert T. Armistead.

48

Residences outside the Historic Area

All these dwellings outside the Historic Area are used as offices or homes for employees of the Colonial Williamsburg Foundation.

James Galt House, restored, stood on property owned by the Commonwealth of Virginia and was moved in order to save the building.

Rabon House, early nineteenth century, unrestored.

Powell-Hallam House, probably built by Benjamin Powell about 1755. It was moved in 1928 to make way for a bypass road around Williamsburg and is now located on Tyler Street.

Griffin House, about 1770, unrestored, now houses Colonial Williamsburg offices. It has many interesting original interior details.

Outbuildings

It is remarkable that so many of these small structures survived. They were less substantial than the residences, and usually did not last as long. Those that remain tell us much about the life and customs of early Williamsburg, and typical examples have made possible the accurate reconstruction of other small buildings.

All of these outbuildings were built separately and each served a special function.

Archibald Blair Kitchen, of the early nineteenth century. Kitchens were built at some distance from the houses to minimize the danger of fire and to keep the residences free of heat and cooking odors.

George Reid Well House.

Robert Carter Brick Quarters, probably built in the third quarter of the eighteenth century, housed family servants.

Bassett Hall Smokehouse. The family meat supply was cured and stored in such buildings. Hams and bacon sides were hung from the rafters and smoked for several days above smoldering fires built on the earthen floors. Walls were unusually strong and locks were stout, to guard against theft.

Tayloe Storehouse.

Tayloe Smokehouse.

52

Powell-Waller Kitchen.

Archibald Blair Dairy, of typical design. Encircling grille work and wide overhang with coved plastered eaves were designed to keep milk products cool.

George Reid Smokehouse.

Archibald Blair Privy, a two-door model.

Franklin Street Kitchen, partly restored. Now used as an employee's residence. It is outside the Historic Area after being moved in order to preserve it.

Brush-Everard Smokehouse.

William Lightfoot Smokehouse.

Powell-Waller Dairy.

Bassett Hall Dairy.

Wetherburn's Dairy, which was moved during the eighteenth century and converted into a smokehouse and later enlarged as part of a residence. It now stands on its eighteenth-century foundations.

Custis-Maupin Necessary.

55

Bassett Hall Kitchen.

Powell-Waller Smokehouse.

William Lightfoot Dairy.

56

Dr. Barraud Privy.

Brush-Everard Kitchen.

Archibald Blair Smokehouse,
with the Dairy at left.

58

Semple Quarter.

Custis Kitchen, early nineteenth century.

Benjamin Waller Smokehouse.

Tunnel entrance to the Palace Icehouse.

Moody Smokehouse.

Bracken Smokehouse.

Coke-Garrett Privy.

Charlton Smokehouse.

Offices

Williamsburg offices served varied and utilitarian purposes. Doctors, lawyers, apothecaries, and merchants built them adjacent to their homes to separate business functions from their household routines. Others used offices as places to conduct business, while some were used as small residences apart from the main house.

Tayloe Office. The rare bell-shaped roof was usually seen on garden buildings as a decorative feature.

Powell-Waller Office, early nineteenth century.

Nelson-Galt Office.

Greenhow-Repiton Office.

Coke-Garrett Office, early nineteenth century, probably used as a doctor's office during the 1800s.

Stores and Shops

These retail outlets served customers from all parts of Virginia, and dealt mostly in goods imported from England. Locally produced merchandise was of limited importance, though the work of colonial craftsmen was sometimes offered for sale.

Taliaferro-Cole Shop, where in 1782 Charles Taliaferro advertised a variety of goods for sale at his "store opposite the Church wall."

Nicolson Shop, with
living quarters overhead.
Robert Nicolson, who
bought the property in
1773, had both a tailor
shop and store here.

Prentis Store, built in 1738-1740, is one of the oldest surviving stores in Williamsburg.

Margaret Hunter Shop, dating from about 1745, was opened as a millinery shortly after 1770.

Taverns

During sessions of the General Assembly and the Court, the overcrowded taverns of the small capital became social and political centers of the Virginia colony. More than a score of places operated as taverns and catered to crowds during Publick Times. Most were located near the Capitol.

Wetherburn's Tavern, where Henry Wetherburn, perhaps Williamsburg's most successful innkeeper, began to serve the public in the 1740s. The tavern was the site of auctions, balls, business conferences, and political meetings. Governor Dinwiddie was entertained here upon his arrival in Williamsburg. Even after Wetherburn's death in 1760, his establishment retained its popularity. Washington frequently dined in the building.

Market Square Tavern, where Jefferson lived for a time while
studying law. The section to the left is original.

The distinctive chimney caps of the
Public Records Office with sloping
weatherings, rubbed brick, and
glazed headers.

Details

The architecture of Williamsburg is relatively simple, and this simplicity is the basis of its esthetic appeal today. By contrast, the details of finish vary from the simple to the highly ornate. These highlights of the town's architecture lend individuality to the buildings and display the considerable skills of eighteenth-century craftsmen. The knowing visitor who studies Williamsburg architecture tends to concentrate on these details.

The molded-brick belt course of the Lightfoot House, showing the contrast of simple details with ornamental ironwork, rubbed brick, and imported glass.

A pedimented gable at the Semple House. The larger blocks are modillions and the smaller blocks are dentils.

An original painted yellow pine end board on the Palmer House, finished in simple curves.

Pedimented dormers of the Benjamin Waller House show an unusual arrangement of horizontal weatherboards. An original lightning rod remains on the chimney.

70

The tall and imposing Bracken House chimney from an unexpected angle. The masonry is protected by three series of sloped weatherings.

A cornice of the Public Records Office. The modillions, basically original, are made in striking S-shape. The lower molding is original.

The Benjamin Waller House with its old rakeboard reveals another method of treating the end of the cornice without an ornamental end board.

The nineteenth-century Greek Revival porch of the Archibald Blair House, added to the eighteenth-century building after 1810.

71

The rather ornate marble mantel in the Great Room of Wetherburn's Tavern. Many initials have been carved into the stone since it was put into place about 1750.

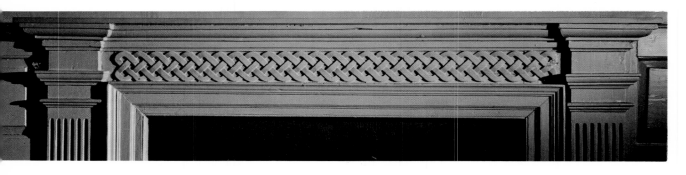

Designs for these original eighteenth-century mantels in the Griffin House (above) and the Semple House were both copied from architectural handbooks of the period. Details of the mantel above were carved by hand and the one at left is sawn fretwork, which has been applied.

An interesting wooden mantel in the James Geddy House rendered by a craftsman in a style to simulate marble masonry. The flooring of edge-grain heart yellow pine is original to the house.

The cheeks of this Waller House fireplace are made of stone panels that appear to have been intended for tombstones.

73

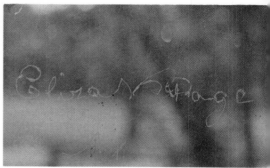

Williamsburg's old glass tells stories of its own. An interior door in the Nicolson Shop, *above,* once divided the shop from the owner's private counting room. Footnotes to history were etched in windowpanes of the Brush-Everard House. The three-masted bark, *upper right,* was probably drawn with a diamond by H. B. Smith, November 17, 1873. Smith was probably a brother of Misses Cora and Estelle Smith, from whom Colonial Williamsburg acquired the house. The lower signature is apparently that of Eliza Page, a relative of Governor John Page, whose widow occupied the house early in the nineteenth century. *Below,* three original windows remaining in Wetherburn's Tavern with most of their original glass.

Painted pine paneling in the Peyton Randolph parlor, with the contrast of natural walnut window trim.

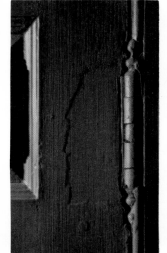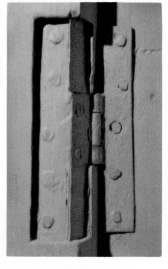

An unusual natural finish of yellow pine paneling in the Market Square Tavern.

Representative examples of original Williamsburg hardware. *Above* and *right center.* A butterfly hinge and an offset H-hinge from an interior shutter of the George Wythe House.

Center left. A painted brass dovetail door hinge at the Semple House.

Below. An iron rim lock on an upstairs closet, Robert Carter House.

A variety of original stairs still in use. It was in the finish of such stairways that ornamentation blossomed forth in Williamsburg's buildings.

OPPOSITE PAGE:

Upper left. The closed-string stairway of the Taliaferro-Cole House. (The balusters do not rest upon the treads.)

Upper right. The open-string stairs at the Griffin House frame the only original archway of its kind in Williamsburg, a design common in eighteenth-century England.

Lower left. The Brush-Everard House stairs with ornate carved brackets remarkably similar to those at Carter's Grove plantation.

Lower right. The "Chinese Chippendale" balustrade in the stairway of the west wing of the Coke-Garrett House.

Above. Sturdy, and simple construction was concealed beneath these ornamental stairways as this view from the Robert Carter House reveals.

Right. The open-string staircase of the George Wythe House with scroll-cut brackets—a stair used by Washington when he made the house his headquarters before the siege of Yorktown.

The pyramid steps of the John Blair House with worn stones held in place by wrought-iron cramps—U-shaped fasteners surrounded by lead.

The curved stone steps of the Nicolson House. The barred basement window is typical of eighteenth-century construction.

The remarkable "cornerstone" of the chapel of the Wren Building of the College of William and Mary. The legend " R K 1729" carved into an original brick after its firing is thought to commemorate Richard Kennon, rector of the Board of Visitors of the College at the time this wing was built. This upside-down brick was found to be in its original position by architectural investigations.